10.95

How to Take Care of Your Voice
The Lifestyle Guide for Singers and Talkers

ISBN-13 978-1-60145-256-6
ISBN-10 1-60145-256-X

Printed in the United States of America.

Note to the reader: The information in this book is offered for educational purposes only. Any and all suggestions and recommendations are intended to supplement, not to replace, professional, individualized medical care. Always consult with your own physician or other licensed, appropriately qualified health-care practitioner.

Booklocker.com, Inc.
2007

www.voiceofyourlife.com

How to Take Care of Your Voice

The Lifestyle Guide for Singers and Talkers

Joanna Cazden, MFA, MS-CCC

ACKNOWLEDGEMENTS

I have learned so much from so many people that it is certain some names will be neglected. Nevertheless here are many who have contributed to this book, but bear no blame for my errors.

Thanks to my parents for filling our home with music, language, humanism, and common sense. To my first voice teachers—theater director Kitty Miller, singer Ellalou "Pete" Dimmock, and choral master Thomas Vasil—for a safe, healthy start. To the theater professors of the University of Washington, ACT, and CalArts, for their liberating disciplines of voice, speech, and body. To Judy Trost-Cardamone, Nancy Sedat, Carol Kysar Shaw, Linda Gasson, Sherry Washington, and the other speech-language pathologists who have encouraged and mentored me. To the laryngologists who have trusted me with their patients and shared their knowledge —especially Drs. David Alessi, Michel Babajanian, Gary Bellack, Mark Courey, Matthew Finerman, Garrett Herzon, Martin Hopp, Babak Larian, Warren Line, Rafi Mesrobian, Madison Richardson, Robert Sataloff, Lorraine Smith, Hans Von Leden, and Mani Zadeh. To all of my patients and students, for reminding me what's important in the human condition. To my present voice teacher Catherine Fitzmaurice for wisdom and generosity. To Vianna Stibal and Theta healing, for accelerated growth in all dimensions. To my husband Scott Wilkinson—partner in life, writing, music, and science—for generous editing and for understanding why I sit at the computer too long.

Thanks above all to the Source of all creation: who sustains us, who keeps us in life, and who brings us to this moment of good.

TABLE OF CONTENTS

It is through our desires, our sensations, our perceptions, that we gain control of our activities in body and mind. This is especially true in singing. ...A friend, a book, a word, a look may help or harm us. ...We find by experience what is hurtful or helpful.

Giovanni Battista Lamperti (1830-1910)

INTRODUCTION

This book is for voice students and those receiving rehabilitative voice care. It is also intended to help prevent voice problems in people who may not think of themselves as vocal professionals.

Teachers, broadcasters, clergy, lawyers, and business and marketing personnel all rely on effective communication, in person and/or on the telephone. Parents and others who care for young children also use their voices constantly, and sometimes loudly, throughout the day.

If you talk and/or sing for hours every day, you are a vocal athlete. Your voice needs good care and maintenance to keep it working well.

I've seen hundreds of voice students and voice-therapy patients over the years, and I am asked the same simple questions over and over. "What should I drink?" "What should I eat?" "Is it true that…?" One purpose of this book is to offer answers to these questions in a convenient package, allowing voice students and their teachers to concentrate on the deeper aspects of training.

The voice is central to human life and society. In public and private, speech and song carry important messages about individual and group identity. The voice is also intricate in its mechanism, virtually out of sight, largely unconscious, and impossible to understand fully when not in use!

Singers and singing teaches have historically led the effort to understand the vocal mechanism. But detailed medical and scientific knowledge in this area became possible only with the sound and imaging technologies of the mid-20th century. Voice care is now an interdisciplinary field that, at its best, unites laryngology, speech science, neurology, speech-language pathology, and artistic voice training.

Recent advances in fiber-optic endoscopy and digital sound processing have led to a rapid explosion of scientific and medical discoveries about the voice. Brain-imaging technologies now promise even more exciting glimpses into how we talk and sing.

Nevertheless, formal voice care is younger than better-known medical specialties like cardiology or sports medicine. There is still a great need for basic public education, which is another primary purpose for the book.

Sources

This lifestyle guide brings together what I've learned about day-to-day voice care through more than 30 years as a voice student, performer, teacher, speech pathologist, and curious reader. Suggestions come from doctors, practitioners of alternative health care, patients, and from my own experiences with health and healing.

It is impossible to cover everything that might be relevant. It is also impossible to anticipate the changes in treatment that will certainly appear as voice-care research continues. Some aspects of vocal health care remain open to argument, even among doctors and scientists, and I don't claim ultimate expertise or infallibility.

Nevertheless, the self-care principles offered here are generally supported by the physicians with whom I've had the privilege to work. Please use what helps you and fits your life, and use the general guidelines to develop your own creative solutions to everyday problems. At the back of the book are resources to help you find more individualized medical care for your voice.

By making sensible choices and developing daily habits that help your voice, you can reduce many of the risks of voice overuse. Knowing how to take care of your voice can also decrease the sense of mystery and uncertainty that sometimes surrounds the voice, helping you feel confident and relaxed wherever you choose to speak or sing.

The goal, after all, is to express yourself using an instrument that just happens to be one of the most fascinating, inspiring parts of the human body-mind-spirit. So get yourself a drink of water, and we'll begin.

A defective voice will always preclude an artist from achieving the complete development of his art, however intelligent he may be. ...The voice is an instrument which the artist must learn to use with suppleness and sureness, as if it were a limb.

Sarah Bernhardt (1845–1923)

Chapter One

FOUNDATIONS OF VOICE CARE

If you want to learn how to take good care of your voice, it helps to start by understanding what it is and how it works. Put aside, for a moment, the idea that the voice produces sound. Of course, the sounds we make in talking and singing are central to our self-expression and to relationships with others. You are probably reading this book because you care about how your voice sounds.

But there is more to it. The voice box, or *larynx* (pronounced "LAA-rinks," not "LAHR-nix"), is essential to our survival. It is an amazing little structure that protects the lungs and airway, and it helps to regulate the flow of air in and out of the body.

How the Voice is Built

The larynx is a framework of cartilage about the size of a walnut. Its most visible landmark is the point of the "Adam's apple" in your throat. It is right in front of your *esophagus* (the passage to your stomach) and its lowest support ring rests on the *trachea* (windpipe).

Inside the larynx are two small folds of flexible tissue, about one centimeter long, running from front to back. These vocal folds are often called the vocal "cords" or, sometimes, the vocal "bands," but if you were inside the throat, looking down, they would look like little shelves.

These vocal folds are made of small muscles, covered first with a slightly stiff layer of cells and then with a very loose, moist mucous membrane similar to the pink lining of your mouth. This moist layer or lining starts above the larynx, in your throat, and it merges below into the lining of the windpipe and the bronchial tubes that branch down into your lungs.

How the Voice Works

Meeting together at the front of the larynx, but attached separately to even smaller bits of cartilage at the back, the vocal folds can be positioned close together or farther apart. Like a flat curtain between rooms, or the valve on the end of a plumbing pipe, these open or closed positions affect the flow of air in and out of the body.

When the vocal folds pivot apart, a triangular space appears between them, and the airway is open. This space—the opening between the vocal folds—is called the *glottis*. When you take in a deep, silent gulp of air or inhale deeply to enjoy the scent of a perfume or favorite food, the glottis is wide open, and the vocal folds are farthest apart.

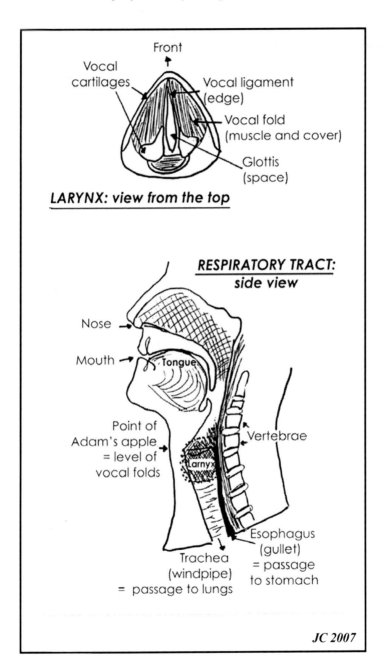

Front

Vocal cartilages

Vocal ligament (edge)

Vocal fold (muscle and cover)

Glottis (space)

LARYNX: view from the top

RESPIRATORY TRACT: side view

Nose

Mouth

Tongue

Point of Adam's apple = level of vocal folds

Larynx

Vertebrae

Esophagus (gullet) = passage to stomach

Trachea (windpipe) = passage to lungs

JC 2007

When you hold your breath tightly, the vocal folds squeeze together and some other structures nearby help to make the seal secure. This happens routinely every time you swallow and can sometimes happen fast enough to keep dust, smoke, or airborne chemicals out of your lungs.

Moving quickly between these open and closed positions also helps to actively clean the airway. The vocal folds can clap together to "clear your throat," or bang together more vigorously during a cough to expel extra phlegm or other stuff that gets into your airway by mistake.

How Your Voice Makes Sound

Between the two extremes of being far apart and closed tightly together, the vocal folds can close part way, reducing the breath stream without completely stopping it. This causes turbulence in the air, and the result is a whooshing, breathy sound—what you hear when someone whispers.

In order to make a normal vocal sound, the vocal folds move into a position where their edges just barely touch. Small support muscles set up a mild amount of elastic tension. Then, when a constant, smooth stream of air from the lungs flows out between the vocal folds, they vibrate and make an audible tone. This act of producing sound, coordinating the vocal muscles with the flow of breath, is formally called *phonation,* from the Greek root "phon," which means sound.

Tiny adjustments within the larynx can make the vocal folds longer and thinner (higher pitch) or shorter and thicker (lower pitch), much like a rubber band. Since the vocal folds are made of muscle, they can be internally tensed or relaxed. They also react automatically to the force, steadiness, and timing of the airflow. (This is why vocalists typically spend considerable time and attention on training the breath, a large topic far beyond the scope of this book.) Altogether, these adjustments create the loudness, pitch, sound quality, and emotional tone of the voice.

How Voice Skills Develop

When a baby is born, everyone waits for its first cry to be sure of its health and strength. Obviously, raw phonation is natural and needs no special training! But the baby isn't able to control the muscles of its breath, voice, throat, and mouth in order to make specific sounds. Appropriately, the word "infant" is Latin for "the speechless one."

Vocal skills begin to develop within the first few months of life. Babies typically spend many hours babbling, exploring a wide variety of cries, sighs, consonants, and melodies. Through this early vocal play, each of us learns to control the position, length, thickness, and internal tension of the vocal folds.

A normal toddler doesn't consciously know how those controls work when he or she is talking. It just happens. We learn that different sounds have different effects on the people around us. Communicating with sounds and words helps us get our needs met. So we learn to use the voice, and then spoken language, for many different purposes.

In early childhood, as our speech becomes more complex, we rely on our voices to carry messages of what we want, how we feel, and to comment or ask about things and events around us. We copy the melody of the language spoken around us, its resonance and inflection. We learn that some situations need a loud voice and others need very quiet sound.

Invisibly, the larynx and breath mechanism become skilled at all these variations. As we mature into adulthood, each individual's muscle habits, personality, life experience, and education combine with the size and shape of their throat to produce a vocal sound that is as unique as a fingerprint. Those of us who use our voices in public learn to produce sound with even more precision, range, power, efficiency, and nuance. When the larynx and breathing mechanisms work together effectively, our loudness, phrasing, pitch inflection, and tone of voice perfectly carry the meaning of what we think and how we feel.

> Speech is power: speech is to persuade, to convert, to compel. It is to bring another out of his bad sense into your good sense.
>
> *Ralph Waldo Emerson (1803–1882)*

Why Good Voices Go Bad

The edges of the vocal folds are stiffened by whitish ligaments. With overuse or injury, these edges can become bruised, irregular, swollen, or scarred. When irritated or inflamed (a condition called *laryngitis*), the vocal folds themselves may appear thicker or unusually red to a doctor's examination.

Under these conditions, the vocal folds may not close as smoothly, open as far, or vibrate as easily as they should. The sound of the voice may become lower in pitch, huskier in tone, softer in volume, harder to control, and/or more tiring to produce.

Other problems in health or usage can make the vocal folds paralyzed, stiff, or weak. They can be taken over by cancer, fungal and viral infections, or bruised by direct injuries to the throat.

Medical conditions that affect the nervous system, fluid level, air supply, or other aspects of our biology, as well as side effects of treatment for various diseases, can also get in the way of good vocal function. *Most voice problems, however, are related to how—and how much—the voice is being used, and most are relatively simple to treat.*

At Best, You Feel Nothing

The vocal muscles are designed to be unconscious. They don't contain the same movement sensors that most other muscles do. That's why, under normal circumstances, you can't feel exactly where they are or how they are working.

Similarly, when something goes wrong, the vocal folds don't send detailed messages back to the conscious mind. Instead, they get your attention with a small repertoire of sensations: a tickle, a cough, a general feeling of tension, effort, or pain.

It is impossible to diagnose the voice accurately by feeling or sound. A particular change in sound or inner sensation can have many different causes and require very different treatments.

This is why, whenever you are concerned about your voice, it is important to get a visual medical exam. See Chapter Six for general information on medical care, and the References section for some online sources of reliable medical referrals.

Start Making Sense

Now you know the fundamentals. Your voice is produced by a small muscular valve near the top of your airway, surrounded and protected by a "box" of cartilage. This voice box is lined with a moist, delicate membrane.

The vocal folds regulate the flow of air, both in and out of the body, and, in turn, they are affected by the amount, force, speed, and chemical quality of the airflow. They can be adjusted into a wide variety of positions and degrees of tension.

Under normal circumstances, the voice does its jobs automatically and unconsciously. It is therefore easy to take our voices for granted until something goes wrong. But this is not enough for a serious student of speech or singing. Just as you check a car's gas, oil, and tires periodically, it is a good idea to perform regular maintenance to keep your voice in good working order, rather than to wait for a big problem.

The suggestions in this book will help you keep your voice healthy and recover when trouble strikes. I have tried to provide enough general principles and references that you can find—and invent—even more answers on your own.

Sound is naught but broken air: and every speech that is uttered, aloud or privily, good or ill, is in substance nothing but air.

Geoffrey Chaucer (1340–1400)

Chapter Two

AIR, STEAM, AND SMOKE

Our lives depend on having air to breathe and water to nourish every cell in our bodies. These elements are also centrally important to keeping your voice healthy.

As I've already explained, the vocal folds vibrate in response to a stream of air flowing out of the body. The voice box and the upper breathing areas (known as the *upper respiratory tract*) also filter the air coming *into* the body.

Inside your nose is a curly "obstacle course" lined with moist mucous membranes. These membranes contain thousands of microscopic hairs (*cilia*) whose job is to catch dust, allergens, and anything else that could hurt your lungs. Ideally, by the time air gets to the last mechanical gateway—the voice box—it is warm, humid, and filtered.

Should I Breathe Through My Nose or Mouth?

I'm often asked this question. Breathing through the nose allows for the filtering I've just described, and it may be subtly more relaxing to the nervous system. Using nose and mouth together obviously helps to take in a larger amount of air, and this is definitely needed during exercise, dance, or other physical exertion. Some singing teachers emphasize inhaling through the nose as a way of opening the upper throat for resonance.

Not everyone has an easy time of this, however. An individual's nasal passages may be structurally small, congested (swollen) from allergies or illness, or partially clogged by dust or other debris. If nasal breathing isn't possible for you on a given day, breathe through your mouth and take extra care to get enough moisture into the air (more about this below). Sip water constantly so that your mouth and throat don't get dry.

Here is a trick that can help keep your larynx moist while breathing through your mouth. Whenever you have a moment to rest between words or phrases, or between songs during a concert, lift the tip of your tongue into an "L" position. This position offers more wet surface area to incoming air. Even a few breaths this way can temporarily ease a dry throat.

In the meantime, do not waste energy or anxiety about whether it is "wrong" to breathe through your mouth. Air is important enough to your survival that your body is built to breathe in more than one way. Trust that your unconscious systems will use what works best with the instrument you have.

Nose Problems

If you have chronic problems with your nose or sinuses, see an ear-nose-throat doctor. Healthy airways are important for your vocal goals, and a low-level, chronic infection in the upper airway can increase the risk of laryngeal inflammation. Refer to Chapter Seven for more information.

If you consult with a doctor who recommends sinus surgery, ask about the impact on your voice. Nasal or sinus surgery rarely affects the vocal folds directly, but it can change your resonance (the enriching vibrations that are amplified in your face and head).

Following nose or sinus surgery, your voice may sound or feel quite different to you, and these changes may not match the feedback you get from other people. Sensations of sound and resonance may not stabilize for several weeks, as you recover from the immediate effects of surgery. A good voice teacher or speech pathologist can help rebalance your sound.

> All things share the same breath—the beast, the tree, the man, they all share the same breath.
>
> *Chief Seattle (c. 1784–1866)*

Moisture in the Airway

Chapter Four will discuss water as a beverage. But moisture in the air is important as well. Since the vocal folds are part of the airway, water vapor in the air you breathe keeps the surfaces of the larynx comfortable.

In humid climates, this is no problem. In dry climates or environments with air conditioning or central heat, your voice will be happier if you add humidity. If your skin gets dry, the lining of your airway will be dry as well. I have talked to many clients whose voices feel and sound better in Hawaii than in Los Angeles!

There are many ways to increase humidity and soothe your voice with moisture. Take extra-long showers when your voice is under stress and at night after a long day of talking or singing. If you have access to a steam room at your gym, health club, or apartment building, use it. (Dry sauna is *not* recommended for this purpose.)

Inexpensive appliances called "facial spas" or "facial steam spas" work very well for the voice. Some performers travel with one in their luggage. Use it daily or whenever you feel the need for extra vocal care (between rehearsal and performance, before hair and makeup, can be a great time.) Or just sit under a towel with your face over a pot of hot water or tea when you feel your voice getting tired.

In addition to more focused steam treatments, using a humidifier or vaporizer next to your bed can very helpful. It should be filled with water only, *not* mentholated ointments or aromatherapy oils. Your doctor may advise a cool-air or warm-air device. Either will serve the purpose of moisturizing the vocal folds. ***To avoid mold contamination, keep the device clean by following the manufacturer's instructions.***

Be creative, especially if you are concerned about cost. In Los Angeles, where I live, the climate is usually hot and dry, and not everyone can afford good air conditioning. One summer, I worked with a singer who complained that her mouth and throat often felt dry in the mornings. She soon explained that in the hot weather, she could sleep only with a fan blowing close to the bed.

After we talked about the importance of a humid airway, she simply kept a bowl of water in front of the fan. Like wind carrying clouds or rain, the fan now blew moisture over her face at night, and she was soon free of that morning discomfort.

Airway Allergies

Respiratory allergies occur when the immune system overreacts to substances encountered in the airway. You may be more affected at certain times of the year or in specific environments. These sensitivities typically begin in childhood or on relocation to a new city.

In addition to learning how to avoid the things that trigger allergies, and strengthening your whole system to be less sensitive, many vocal performers use air filters or purifiers at home as a precaution. There is no one type of purifier that I recommend, but a clean environment is generally helpful for a healthy voice.

A CAUTIONARY TALE

Once upon a time, a singing student from overseas carefully saved enough money to travel, attend music school in the USA, and study with a particular teacher whom she had read about online. This student suffered from an allergy to cats. She could not have known, while preparing for her journey, that the teacher who ran the school always kept cats in his vocal studio. This teacher required all beginning students to work with him.

Week after week, the student went to her singing lessons, always leaving the studio with watery, itchy eyes and extra phlegm in her nose and throat. She would cough for days afterwards, and after a couple of months, she became totally unable to breathe through her nose. Her voice gradually became hoarse, and she lost her highest notes.

She asked to take her private lessons in a different building, away from the cats, but was refused. If she dropped any of her classes, she would lose her student visa. She had sacrificed a lot for her training, and she was miserable.

After a few months, the student was diagnosed with vocal nodules (calluses), probably due to the vigorous coughing brought on by the allergies. Only then did the school director take her concerns seriously. She was allowed to take individual lessons with another teacher.

It took about six months for this young singer to get back her full range and her pleasure in singing. One wonders: If a teacher does not understand or respect vocal health, how can he or she be trusted to train healthy technique?

Where There's Smoke

Cigarette smoking—now banned in many public places, but still common in others, as well as in private—is well known to contribute to serious health problems, including cancer, heart disease, high blood pressure, and emphysema. Tobacco smoke also contains chemicals that damage the cells inside the voice box.

Inhaled smoke is burning hot, which traumatizes the vocal folds with every puff. After just a few months of regular cigarette use, the mucous membranes inside the voice box become yellow-stained from nicotine, just like the fingers that hold the cigarettes.

Over time, exposure to the heat and chemicals in cigarette smoke makes the vocal folds inflamed and swollen with extra fluid as the body tries to protect itself. The voice sounds rough and low-pitched, and the vocal folds may become damaged by frequent, persistent coughing.

Just like the nose, the windpipe (*trachea*) and bronchial tubes of the lower airway are lined with mucous membranes and with microscopic hairs called *cilia*. These cells have the job of clearing germs and debris out of the lungs.

Hot chemical smoke paralyzes the cilia, so they can't do their protective job. As a result, smokers are more likely to get bronchitis and other respiratory illnesses.

It is VERY IMPORTANT for vocalists not to smoke! Use any and all available tools, medications, support groups, and online clubs to help you quit. It often takes several tries to extinguish this habit permanently, so if you relapse, don't give up—look for even more support.

If you don't smoke but often perform in smoky settings, the other health ideas in this book will help to protect your voice and to recover quickly from smoke-related irritation.

Chapter Two Supplement

QUITTING SMOKING

The Stages of Quitting Smoking

1. *Precontemplation:* no desire to quit.
2. *Contemplation:* a desire to quit but no quitting plan.
3. *Preparation:* a desire to quit within one month and a plan.
4. *Action:* the person has quit for one day to six months.
5. *Maintenance:* the person has quit for at least six months.

www.drugdigest.org/DD/HC/Treatment/0,4047,850,00.html

How Your Body Recovers When You Quit

- 20 minutes after the last cigarette: heart rate drops.
- 12 hours after the last cigarette: the carbon monoxide level in the blood returns to normal.
- 2 weeks to 3 months after the last cigarette: circulation improves and lung function increases.

- 1 to 9 months after the last cigarette: coughing and shortness of breath decrease; cilia begin to function normally again, increasing the ability to clean out the lungs and thus reduce the risk for lung infection.
- 1 year after the last cigarette: risk of heart disease is decreased by half compared to a smoker's risk.
- 5 years after the last cigarette: risk for having a stroke is the same as a person who never smoked.
- 10 years after the last cigarette: lung cancer death rate is about half of a smoker's. The risk of cancer of the mouth, throat, esophagus, bladder, cervix, and pancreas decreases as well.
- 15 years after the last cigarette: the risk of heart disease is the same as a person who never smoked.

The Surgeon General's 1990 Report on the Health Benefits of Smoking Cessation
www.cdc.gov/mmwr/preview/mmwrhtml/00001799.htm

The best doctors in the world are Doctor
Diet, Doctor Quiet, and Doctor Merryman.
Jonathan Swift (1667–1745)

Chapter Three

FOOD

You Don't Talk Where You Swallow

Your mouth and throat lead into the pathways for both breathing and swallowing. Look back at the illustration in Chapter One: The passages to the lungs and the digestive tract are very close together at the back of the throat, but at that point they divide and remain separate. Your larynx serves as the switching station between these pathways, as part of its biological job of protecting the airway.

Most of the time, your airway is open and your esophagus (the tube from your throat to your stomach) is closed. When it's time to swallow something—food, liquid, medicine, or normal saliva—strong, inborn reflexes keep the larynx closed so that what you swallow doesn't "go down the wrong way."

Put simply, *under normal circumstances, nothing that you eat or drink directly touches the vocal folds.* Nevertheless, the pathways for eating and breathing/voicing are so close together that it is easy to believe or imagine that you can make your voice sound or feel better by drinking or eating something.

This is one instance where common sense is wrong. In general, you should choose what to eat or drink based on overall health, rather than what might feel good in your throat.

There are three main ideas to keep in mind about nutrition for a healthy voice. These are general stamina, precautions against acid reflux, and keeping the digestive system comfortable rather than over-stuffed.

Smart Fuel

A healthy voice requires general strength and stamina. So plan a balance of protein, fruits and vegetables, whole grains and beans, and moderate amounts of healthy fats and oils. There are plenty of books and beliefs about the best way to select food; see "Body, Mind, and Breath" books in the References section for a few respected guides to holistic health.

In my experience, individual bodies vary. Some people feel energized by protein rather than carbohydrate fuel, while others feel weighed down by meat and prefer lighter fare. Pay attention to how *you* feel and experiment until you find a food regimen that suits your own body, schedule, and budget. Consult with a dietician or nutritionist for individualized help..

Your Throat on Acid

As shown in the illustration in Chapter One, the larynx is so close to the esophagus that only a few layers of tissue separate them. If a small amount of stomach acid sneaks back up the esophagus (a process called *reflux*), it is likely to "land" at the back area of the vocal cords.

Although the breathing and swallowing tubes are close to each other, they lined with different kinds of cells. The inside of the digestive system has special buffers against the strong acids and other materials that do the work of digestion. The inside of the larynx and lower airway don't have this protection. Any acid material from the stomach will irritate or burn them.

When this wash of acid affects the larynx, it is called *laryngo-pharyngeal reflux*, or *LPR*. One such episode can have effects on the voice that last for days, and repeated episodes over time can cause chronic vocal changes and/or discomfort.

Some voice patients with reflux irritation report stomach discomfort, burning sensations, acidic taste in the mouth, and so on, but most do not. It is very important to emphasize that *acid-related vocal inflammation often occurs without any familiar symptoms of heartburn.* Sometimes termed "silent reflux", its main symptoms are in the voice and throat.

Common complaints associated with laryngeal reflux include a gradual roughening of the voice that seems independent of overuse or any lingering cold, and the sensation of a thickening or lump in the throat, as if there's "something in there." Throat-clearing often increases but brings little relief.

A singer's midrange may become harder to control, in contrast with other vocal problems that tend to hurt the upper range first. In more serious or chronic cases of laryngeal reflux, the voice can sound low-pitched and crackly, and it can feel tired more easily.

These are complaints that I hear from numerous patients with this diagnosis. But not everyone has the same symptoms, and it is important to repeat that you *cannot* diagnose your own voice problems by sound or feel.

A doctor will make the clinical diagnosis of *reflux laryngitis*—or not— based on the appearance of your vocal folds on a visual exam, your symptoms, and whether certain medications make your voice and throat better. Possible symptoms or complaints are mentioned here so that, if you experience these things, you can describe them to your doctor. If anti-reflux medications are effective in resolving your throat symptoms, the diagnosis is confirmed.

Acid reflux is more common in women than men, in people over age 35, and in those who are overweight. Ironically, singers and vigorous talkers are believed to be at increased risk for laryngo-pharyngeal reflux. Scientists don't yet know why.

If laryngeal reflux is left untreated, more serious throat problems can develop over time, such as a benign but painful sore on one or both vocal cords (*granuloma*). In the most extreme cases, uncontrolled acid reflux can contribute to laryngeal cancer.

Most of the time, laryngeal reflux is mild and easily managed, usually with a combination of medication, diet, and lifestyle changes. If you are diagnosed, your doctor and/or speech pathologist will provide you with specific information.

> He who takes medicine and neglects his diet wastes the skill of his doctors.
>
> *Chinese Proverb*

Anti-Reflux Regimen

Limit or eliminate alcoholic beverages, coffee, citrus and tomato foods and juices, and extremely fatty or spicy foods. (The latest information on coffee is that it may not cause reflux, but it worsens reflux problems that already exist. Decaffeinated coffee and tea appear to be less of a problem.) Soda and other sparkling beverages can increase pressure in the stomach and make reflux episodes more likely. Some doctors and patients recommend staying away from raw onions and garlic. Not all of the research is complete, and different people may have different sensitivities. Over time each person learns what works.

Don't eat late at night; if you have an evening snack, make it small, easily digested, and sit up for a while before going to bed. Depending on the severity of your problem, your doctor may recommend 2-4 hours between food and sleep. If you have no indication of reflux, your voice may still benefit from many of these precautions. Smoking has also been proven to increase the risk of acid reflux. This is one more good reason to quit.

If it feels impossible for you to give up favorite foods and drinks entirely, make gradual changes. Be honest with yourself, do the absolute best you can, and revisit the recommendations frequently to see what's working and what additional improvements you can make in your daily habits.

You may also be instructed to elevate the head of your bed, so that during the night, gravity helps keep stomach juices where they belong. This should be done with blocks under the bed posts or a wedge-shaped pillow. Propping up just your head on extra pillows tends to squeeze the midsection of the body, which defeats the purpose of this technique.

Some holistic-health specialists deny the problem of acid reflux and warn of horrible side effects from the most common anti-reflux medications. It is easy to understand that while the companies who produce and promote these new medications have made acid reflux a household word, they have also triggered a skeptical over-reaction in some circles.

The latest research indicates that if there is no benefit from 3-6 months of treatment with diligent lifestyle changes and the most advanced anti-reflux medications, the problem is probably not reflux. So stay in close touch with your doctor.

Unstuffing

It's important for your digestion to be comfortable and not too full. In the midsection of the body, digestion and breathing can seem to compete for space. Huge meals can make you sluggish, and they also take up space below your diaphragm, making it harder for the breathing muscles to work.

However, not eating at all before a performance or important speech can make you spacey or weak. Small meals and snacks spaced throughout the day may help keep your energy steady and your breath support consistent.

For those who perform at night, it is often tempting—if not ritualized—to eat a large meal after the show. This can feel like a psychological reward as well as a time of social bonding after hard teamwork. But a heavy meal, especially with alcoholic drinks, increases risks of acid reflux and will make it harder to sleep.

Try having a smaller snack after the show (fruit, yogurt, cereal), no alcohol, and finish unwinding with a shower (steam treatment) and meditative breathing exercises. Plan on a bigger breakfast the next morning as your main daily fuel.

Got Milk Worries?

Many voice students are told to avoid milk, cheese, and other dairy products. Usually, the explanation is that milk increases mucous (phlegm). This is not entirely accurate, but it does have a partial basis in reality and may be a concern for some vocalists.

Here is how it was explained to me. The mouth and throat environments contain many chemicals, some of which control the amount and consistency of phlegm. There is one enzyme in particular whose job is to make phlegm thinner and easier to swallow. A protein in cow's milk stops this enzyme from doing its job. This is why phlegm stays thicker when you drink milk or eat cheese and it feels as if there is more of it.

For vocalists, this can mean mild congestion, frequent throat-clearing, and/or duller resonance. So staying away from milk products may be a common-sense adjustment for the voice-protective lifestyle.

I'd just add a few cautions. Some people are more reactive to milk than others, so what works for a friend or teacher may be less important for you.

If you want to know how dairy products actually affect your voice, experiment. Avoid all dairy products for 4-6 hours before a few practice sessions and performances, without changing anything else in your normal routine. If you find that your voice works significantly better in a dairy-free zone, you can choose to make this change part of your normal healthy-voice plan.

Common sense puts dairy foods in context, one element among many that influence your vocal health and performance. If you decide to give up milk, be sure to replace it with other sources of protein and calcium. And since milk products increase the feeling of thick phlegm, it may be wise for everyone to avoid or limit dairy products during a cold.

Other Food Concerns

I occasionally see voice clients who have chronic digestive problems such as irritable bowel syndrome or gastritis. Chronic pain or discomfort in the abdomen often leads these people to unconsciously restrict their breathing. If breathing is shallow, the voice is at risk. For these folks, the waist and abdomen areas often feel like frustrating personal battlegrounds, rather than active, expressive parts of the breath and voice system.

I encourage you to support your voice—an organ connected to so many systems of the body—by taking care of your health in every dimension. If digestive problems make it hard to feel comfortable in your body, to use your breath effectively, or to concentrate on your training, getting help for these conditions may improve your voice over time.

On the other hand, if your voice is generally working well, consider the difference between reasonable food precautions and unnecessary anxiety. I've heard young vocalists agonize about the smallest imperfections in what they eat, when their time and energy could be spent more constructively on vocal practice and on adequate sleep and exercise. Keep the big picture in mind.

Throats burned dry and souls that cry
for water,
Cool water.

Bob Nolan (1908-1980)
Sons of the Pioneers

Chapter Four

DRINK

No Substitute

Most serious talkers and singers have already heard that it's important to drink a lot of water. This water does *not* directly "wet" the vocal folds. As explained in the previous chapter, swallowing water sends it down the other tube, the esophagus, into your stomach.

Drinking plenty of water *does* make sure that the cells inside the voice box are nourished and resilient. If the body as a whole is dehydrated, the vocal folds get tired faster, and they recover more slowly from heavy use.

Recommendations on the right amount of water intake range from "at least 64 ounces or 2 liters per day" to "as much as it takes to pee pale." The latest guideline I've heard is to divide your weight in pounds by 2, and drink that number of ounces. Someone who weighs 160 pounds would aim for 160/2 = 80 ounces (5 pints) of water per day.

As an alternative calculation: Try to drink 1/32 of your body weight in water every day. In the metric system, someone who weighs 64 kg would plan to drink 2 liters per day, and so on.

As always, use common sense. If you have heart or kidney problems, or other concerns about fluid intake, talk to your doctor before making drastic changes.

Sipping water throughout the day and evening is better than trying to drink a lot all at once. Ice-cold drinks used to be forbidden to serious vocalists. However, research has shown that it doesn't matter whether you drink cold, hot, warm, or lukewarm beverages during rehearsal and performance.

Drink whatever temperature you like, what feels best on a particular day. The main thing is to get plenty of fluids on a regular basis.

Coffee and Other Culprits

The beverages to avoid are those that contain alcohol or caffeine, especially coffee. These chemicals draw water out of the body, so they do not count toward your daily water "ration." Eliminate them if you can, or cut back gradually, and drink enough water to compensate.

As explained in the previous chapter, coffee appears to increase the severity of acid reflux. Tea and decaffeinated coffee appear to be safer. Coffee and other caffeinated beverages also disrupt sleep, and they can increase anxiety and stage-fright-related symptoms.

Many of my patients say that they need caffeine boosts because they don't sleep well—but perhaps they are not sleeping well because of drinking so much coffee! Make changes gradually but steadily, and you may feel better than you expect.

I worked with a businessman who complained of vocal fatigue, and he was in the habit of drinking coffee throughout the day. He drank very little water. When he got into the habit of keeping water at his desk, he was surprised at how refreshing it could be.

He found that his voice did not tire out as easily when he sipped water throughout the day and drank less coffee. He slept better, and within a month his energy in general improved so that he felt less need for a caffeine boost, even in the late afternoon.

> But with the dawn I'll wake and yawn
> and carry on to water,
> Cool water.
>
> *Bob Nolan*

Liquid Courage (Not)

Alcoholic beverages are strongly discouraged for the serious voice user. In addition to the risks of reflux and dehydration, alcohol alters your judgment about how loud you are in social settings or when it is time to stop talking or singing.

Despite the romantic mythology about artists, alcohol and drugs are not required for creativity, and they are likely to hurt a long-term career. I'm sorry to sound like an old-fashioned scold, but a healthy lifestyle will give you deeper pleasure in the long run—and a much, much healthier voice.

Soda and Sport Drinks

Carbonated sodas are discouraged by some voice experts, because the extra fullness in the stomach competes with more basic needs for breathing and digestion. Drinking soda before a rehearsal or performance can impair good breath technique, not to mention the risks of belching in the middle of a phrase.

"Energy" or "new-age" drinks are often favored by performing artists and others who feel pressured to work long hours with inadequate rest. These beverages are typically based on sugar and caffeine (sometimes in herbal form, such as guarana), plus herbs or vitamins that promise to increase "pep." But this "energy" is not free—it is borrowed from the future. These drinks can leave you even more tired down the road.

Energy and fitness drinks that advertise weight loss may be lower in sugar but high in potassium, a diuretic, or they may be even higher in caffeine or herbal stimulants. These "energy" herbs may have side effects on sleep or mood. Know what you are putting in your body, and why! If a doctor or other voice professional asks you about drinking coffee, include your energy drinks in the same category.

If these beverages have been in your lifestyle for a long time when you decide to cut back, it may be better to ease off in stages rather than stopping suddenly. For instance, dilute them half and half with water for a couple of weeks, or switch to plain water after lunch. As always, know yourself and what works for you.

Sports drinks are designed to replace sugar and electrolytes (minerals) lost during hard exercise. They are not typically necessary for singers or talkers, unless you also dance for hours every day or exercise heavily.

The newest "vitamin waters" have not been shown to be harmful. However, relying on them for your fundamental nutrition may lead you to eat fewer fruits and vegetables. These fresh foods contain fiber (protective against reflux) and micro-nutrients that are not found in the packaged drinks.

For my voice, I have lost it with halloing
and singing of anthems.

William Shakespeare (1564–1616)
King Henry IV. Part II

Chapter Five

VOICE REST

Even the most talented, best-trained voices need rest. In the early days of voice care, when there was a problem with the voice, doctors would often tell patients to rest it in complete silence for a month or more. In the modern world, guidelines for resting the voice are not usually that extreme.

There are some problems and situations—such as after vocal surgery—when a doctor may still advise a week or two of total voice rest. These instructions are very important to follow, so that the edges of your vocal folds can heal properly.

For the more common vocal problems caused by overuse, a useful guideline is to "talk half as much and half as loud." For instance, eliminate the most intense vocal demands first, and take silence breaks throughout the day. A speech therapist can be especially helpful in analyzing your vocal risks and life demands and suggesting ways to rest.

Even so, reducing voice use can be difficult, given the demands of jobs, school, and family. Isolation from your closest relationships, or fears about not fulfilling job obligations, can interfere with the subtler levels of healing. Employers may need to know that the situation is temporary and that you're willing to take on other responsibilities with less vocal demand.

Friends and family may need multiple reminders about what you are doing. Reassure them that you still care for them, but you need to stay connected without "using up" your voice. Email and text messaging can be extremely helpful.

Especially now that cell phones follow us everywhere, it can be disorienting to stop talking. Plan the important things to say before you make a phone call, and stick to that agenda rather than using hours of telephone chat to fill time or to ease boredom or anxiety.

Once my patients decide to give their voices more rest, many of them are amazed and pleased that their communication actually improves. They learn how to make careful choices about what's important to say and when listening is enough. They also start to value the silent time for reflection and relaxation.

> A field that has rested gives a bountiful crop.
>
> *Ovid (43 B.C. - A.D.17)*

Vocal rest periods are also important *before* trouble strikes as part of general preventative care. This can mean taking short breaks throughout the day, especially if your job requires constant talking (such as teaching, sales, broadcasting, and customer service).

When you have a big vocal demand coming up, build in rest periods before and after. If you have extremely heavy vocal demands (for example, vocal performances every night with all-day rehearsals, business meetings, or a speech-heavy daytime job), try to set aside one full day per week to be silent and let your vocal cords recover.

After all, star athletes have built-in rest days, or they play in rotation. If you are a vocal athlete, your throat needs the same care.

Remember that when your voice needs rest, you can still rehearse mentally, as athletes do. Go through a warm-up routine or performance in your imagination. Quiet days are also a good time to write or edit material, to study texts or music that you need to memorize, or to work on your press kit.

Operatic tenor and conductor Placido Domingo was once asked whether he had a secret way to keep his voice in top form. He answered, "Before a performance, I make sure to sleep 11 hours!"

You may not need that much, but do aim to get 7-8 hours of sleep regularly. The dietary guidelines earlier in this book—minimal caffeine and alcohol, no big meals before bed—will also help you get good-quality sleep.

The office of medicine is but to tune this curious harp of man's body and to reduce it to harmony.

Sir Francis Bacon, 1622

Chapter Six

MEDICAL CARE

When to Go to a Throat Doctor

Serious vocal artists should get a laryngeal checkup every year. According to Hans von Leden, MD, one of the fathers of modern laryngology and a longtime supporter of vocal arts, there are four additional reasons for a vocalist to go to a doctor for a throat exam.

These reasons are: (1) hoarseness or other change in the voice that lasts more than two weeks; (2) a loss of voice or other sudden change that occurs during a performance; (3) pain associated with using the voice; (4) lack of normal progress in voice training as judged by the teacher in comparison to other similar students.

Although your medical care may begin with a visit to your primary or general-practice doctor, the next important step is to be seen by an ear-nose-throat specialist ("ENT" or *otolaryngologist*). Not all ENTs specialize in voice problems, so ideally you should be seen by one who does: a *laryngologist*.

See the Resources section at the end of this book for help finding good-quality medical voice care. The best facilities offer a team approach, including a laryngologist, a speech pathologist, and a singing or artistic speech specialist. These cross-disciplinary voice centers are currently found in many major cities, and their numbers are growing.

Wherever you are able to get care, ideally, you should be examined using an endoscope—a tiny camera inserted through the nose (known as a "flexible scope") or into the mouth (a "rigid" or "fixed scope"). A strobe light and video recorder attached to these instruments provide the best, slow-motion, large-size view of the vocal folds in motion. (This process is called *videostroboscopy*.)

Not all laryngologists or other ENT doctors have invested in this equipment, especially in rural areas or at facilities that are not part of a university or research center. These doctors may be wise and well-meaning, but they will have a harder time making a correct diagnosis.

Common sense says start where you can, and if there is any question about treatment, get a second opinion. Make sure that every doctor you talk to understands that you are a vocal performer.

There are now many websites with extensive information on medical voice care. These sites are great for educating yourself and coming to understand the vocal instrument. See the Online Resources section for some sites that I like. But *please resist the temptation to diagnose yourself.*

I'm sorry to keep repeating this, but it's important: Vocal problems cannot be diagnosed or judged accurately by sound or by how your throat feels to you. There are no good substitutes for a visual exam and individualized care from a laryngologist familiar with the needs of vocalists.

> If you trust Google more than your doctor then maybe it's time to switch doctors.
> *Jadelr and Cristina Cordova*
> *videoblog 08-21-06*

Speech Therapy for the Voice

If you have a voice problem related to how, or how much, you use your voice, or if other medical conditions have caused changes in your voice, the laryngologist may refer you to a speech pathologist. Think of this as physical therapy for your throat.

The speech pathologist will start with a detailed interview to determine your health and vocal habits, along with measurements and analysis of your vocal sound. Some speech pathologists also measure airflow using a special mask while you sing or talk.

As with ear-nose-throat doctors, not all speech pathologists are specialists in voice care. Most, however, can help with the most common vocal problems. Ideally, the laryngologist will send you to someone appropriate.

The goal here is to understand how you *use* your voice—which muscles are overused or not working properly and how your lifestyle and amount of voice use may contribute to the problem. The speech pathologist (sometimes called a speech therapist) then uses voice, breathing, or other exercises to retrain your voice and helps you establish healthier vocal habits.

Speech therapy can be similar to working with a singing or speech coach. However, there are important differences. For example, a speech pathologist has greater medical and scientific knowledge and is formally licensed and accountable for the quality of care provided. Speech pathologists are also required to stay up-to-date in their field through continuing education at conferences and seminars.

Voice teachers are often very skilled and insightful, but they are not legally qualified to work with damaged voices, except in collaboration with a medical team. In the best situations, the speech pathologist has training in the vocal arts and/or works closely with an artistic voice coach.

Most important of all is that you understand your voice and recognize the warning signs of problems: changes in sound or feel, difficulty with power or range. You may also find that your voice is affected by medical conditions that you think are unrelated to the throat.

The voice is very personal, very much inside you, yet it is easy to take for granted until something goes wrong. When you are healthy, work on developing vocal habits that prevent problems. When something does go wrong, or it's time for a checkup, it is better to see a doctor than try to just get by.

If health insurance is a problem, try to save money when you are healthy so you can get voice care when you need it. Talk frankly to the doctors whom you consult; some will be willing to make an accommodation for vocal artists in need.

You'll get the most benefit from your investments in health care by following the recommendations you are given and practicing diligently what you learn. A healthy voice is worth the effort.

Keeping your body healthy is an expression of gratitude to the whole cosmos—the trees, the clouds, everything.

Thich Nhat Hanh (1926 -)

Chapter Six Supplement

VOICE THERAPY, VOICE TRAINING

The Role of the Speech-Language Pathologist, the Teacher of Singing, and the Speaking Voice Trainer in Voice Habilitation (Excerpts)

Since the founding of the American Speech-Language-Hearing Association (ASHA) in 1925, the founding of the National Association of Teachers of Singing (NATS) in 1944, and the founding of the Voice and Speech Trainers Association (VASTA) in 1986, there has been increasing awareness of (a) the importance of having healthy laryngeal function in all styles of speech and singing and (b) the existence of a connection between optimal vocal usage in speech and optimal vocal usage in singing.

... All three organizations acknowledge that the most effective path to vocal recovery often will include an integrated approach to optimal voice care and production that addresses both speech and singing tasks. ASHA, NATS, and VASTA therefore collectively affirm the importance of interdisciplinary management of speakers and singers with voice problems and disorders, with the management team ideally consisting of some or all of the following individuals: an otolaryngologist, a speech-language pathologist, and a singing teacher and/or speaking voice and speech trainer.

....   ASHA, NATS, and VASTA encourage their members to cooperate in the development and delivery of interdisciplinary programs and services for singers and other professional voice users with voice disorders.

American Speech-Language-Hearing Association Technical Report, 2005; see References.

There is plenty of mystery about health and illness without adding to it. I hope physicians of the coming century will be able to acknowledge...that educating patients about prevention and treatment will make their day-to-day jobs significantly easier.

Andrew Weil, MD 1983

Chapter Seven

COLDS

Colds and Laryngitis

In medical jargon, the common cold is called an *upper respiratory infection*, or URI. Serious voice users have the same risk as anyone else for picking up these annoying bugs. But for us, the consequences are more severe, especially if the infection gets into the throat.

Swollen vocal folds vibrate more slowly, which makes vocal pitch lower. The folds may also vibrate unevenly, leading you to sound hoarse or rough. Other vocal symptoms of a URI can include a smaller pitch range, especially the loss of high notes (inflamed cords don't stretch as far) and less control over loudness (that all-or-nothing honk).

Extra congestion in the nose or sinuses can block resonance, making your voice sound dull. Chest congestion or overall fatigue can hurt your breath support. Repeated coughing can irritate otherwise healthy vocal fords.

Under any of these conditions, pushing or tensing to try to sound "normal" will give you more trouble in the long run. Instead, a few days of relative silence—plus sleep, fluids, and steam—will help your voice to recover quickly and help you to avoid compromising your vocal technique.

Dr. Neil Schachter's book, *The Good Doctor's Guide to Colds and Flu*, is full of great information and advice; see References. Some of his suggestions are:

- To keep from getting colds, wash your hands often, and use anti-microbial cleaning sprays on surfaces and objects that others touch, such as car seats, pens, countertops, or telephones.

- At the first sign of a cold, take 500 mg of vitamin C daily; also helpful are zinc nasal spray, swabs, or lozenges and chicken soup. As symptoms develop or linger, continue the above, plus a glass of orange juice, 3-4 cups of hot tea, and plenty of other fluids every day. Take a hot shower every morning to loosen phlegm. Twice per day, use warm water and a bit of salt to gargle (for sore throat) and/or rinse your nasal passages.

- Use a vaporizer or humidifier during the night. Eat light meals for the first few days you are ill. Use over-the-counter remedies for symptomatic relief. Resume a normal diet after a few days.

- If all symptoms are above the neck, it is safe to continue your regular fitness routines. If symptoms involve your chest, take a few days off from vigorous exercise.

- Call your regular doctor if you have trouble breathing, chest pain, or a fever of 102 degrees (F) or higher.

Lozenges and Sprays

Throat lozenges in packages that promise to relieve sore throat pain typically contain menthol, eucalyptus, or benzocaine, which temporarily numb the throat. These lozenges are aromatic, which means you inhale the chemicals as vapors.

Unfortunately, the same chemicals that give temporary relief tend to irritate the vocal folds, making them *more* vulnerable to infection and strain. You are also more likely to overuse your voice if the "stop, it hurts" signals from your throat are numbed out.

There are now many varieties of non-mentholated lozenges. Even simple hard candy will do the job of stimulating saliva to keep your mouth comfortable, and ice chips may help to numb your throat pain without other side effects.

Several over-the-counter mouth sprays are now marketed to vocalists at music, health-food, and drug stores. The main ingredients are typically glycerin or licorice, which may have a mild, temporarily soothing effect on the upper throat but little effect on the larynx itself. (Remember that when you swallow, what's in your mouth goes down the other way.)

There is some evidence that these sprays may irritate the vocal folds. They are also relatively expensive. Call me old-fashioned or skeptical, but I recommend that you spend your money on good nutrition and training instead.

The only mouth sprays intended to touch the vocal folds are prescription inhalants for asthma, allergies, acutely swollen vocal cords, and other respiratory conditions. Follow your doctor's advice when using these medications.

Nasal Irrigation

Rinsing the nasal passages with salt water is a traditional practice in yoga that has become popular in wider communities, and it is favored by many vocalists and ENT doctors. This practice clears "gunk" from the back of the nose, helping the sinuses to drain normally and stay healthy.

In the yoga tradition, a small cup with a long spout called a Neti pot is used, and these are now available online and in many health-food stores and pharmacies.

Some Neti pots are packaged with pre-measured ingredients, usually a mixture of salt and baking soda, occasionally with added zinc or herbal tinctures. These can sting, as can iodized salt. The simplest home recipe is a small pinch of non-iodized table salt and a smaller pinch of baking soda (bicarbonate) per cup of warm water.

Some vocalists perform nasal irrigation every day in their normal bathing routine. Others consider it an extra precaution during cold-and-flu season or at the first sign of a cold. If you are often congested or tend to get sinus infections, you may wish to use nasal irrigation regularly. As always, talk to your doctor about any questions or concerns.

WHAT DO I PUT IN MY TEA?

Tea has earned a reputation as something to drink when you have a cold. Green tea has gotten a lot of praise recently for antioxidant properties. Regular (black) tea turns out to have just as many helpful ingredients, and it is somewhat better at relieving chest congestion.

Any hot beverage, including plain hot water, can help to keep you hydrated, thin out secretions (phlegm), increase circulation in the throat, and send steamy vapors into the airway.

Lemon and/or honey have not been proven to have any particular benefits for the common cold, but they are not harmful either. Use them to taste.

Traditional Medicinals' Throat Coat tea was formally studied in people with colds and sore throat. It relieved more discomfort than the "placebo" tea in the comparison, but only for about 30 minutes.

Many singers favor ginger tea, which warms the throat and eases digestion. Whole ginger (chopped or sliced) can also be added to chicken or vegetable soup for extra warmth.

Remember that milk products increase the feeling of thick phlegm, so if you like tea with milk, in the English style, drink it plain when you have a cold.

If the Show Must Go On

If you simultaneously have a cold and a commitment to perform, the dilemma can be more difficult than your fogged-in brain wants to deal with. Canceling or postponing your audition or show may seem to put at risk your career, school grade, management, friendships, or loyalty to a director.

Common lore advises that established stars and beginners have the most freedom to cancel an appearance without serious consequences. Those at the middle stages of a career or training program are under the most scrutiny—most at risk for being judged unreliable, unavailable, or inadequate.

Talk with your doctor about whether you are risking further vocal damage if you push yourself to perform. It can also be very helpful to consult with someone outside of the immediate pressure cooker—someone who has no agenda in the matter, who cares about your well-being as well as your desire to appear as promised.

There are prescription medications that can knock back an acute laryngeal inflammation in time for an important performance. But don't push your luck by constantly talking, singing, preaching, or shouting when ill.

If you decide to go on, rehearse in shorter sessions, and be extra attentive to your vocal technique. Respect any temporary limits on your pitch range, tone quality, and/or breathing. Maintain the emotional connection to your material, and communicate that meaning even if your sound is less than you hope for.

Drink plenty of fluids, and be especially cautious about exposure to smoke, hairspray, or other irritants. Minimize non-essential talking (such as backstage chatter or extended verbal agonizing about how to handle your illness).

If you need to meet and greet guests before or after the show, stay at the edge of the crowd (less background noise), smile more than you speak, and keep water or tea with you. Shower or steam after the show, before you go to sleep.

I have worked with high-level performing artists who admit that when illness strikes, they tend to repeatedly "test" their voice on the hardest bits of material. This stresses the voice, reinforces habits of tension and anxiety, and disrupts their familiar preparation routine. It is far better to rest as much as you can, then do a normal preparation process in warm-up and rehearsal, even if the result is not perfect.

Pushing yourself to sound normal before you are completely healthy increases the risk of permanent vocal damage.

More commonly, there is a risk of falling into bad habits of tension and other compensations that will be hard to unlearn.

Many voice patients whom I see in the spring or summer trace their problems back to the winter season, when they got a bad cold, became exhausted, but sang and/or talked a lot anyway. Vocalizing with swollen cords and reduced breath support required extra effort and tension, which then became ingrained bad habits.

Six or eight months down the road, these patients found they had deeper voice problems, more anxiety, and larger medical bills that could have been avoided. So even during periods of heavy vocal demand, pay attention to early warning signs, and plan ahead.

A Short History of Medicine

2000 B.C. - "Here, eat this root."

1000 B.C. - "That root is heathen, say this prayer."

1850 A.D. - "That prayer is superstition, drink this potion."

1940 A.D. - "That potion is snake oil, swallow this pill."

1985 A.D. - "That pill is ineffective, take this antibiotic."

2000 A.D. - "That antibiotic is artificial. Here, eat this root."

Author Unknown

Chapter Eight

COMPLEMENTARY AND ALTERNATIVE MEDICINE

Recent news reports show that in the USA, people now use "alternative" remedies and procedures as often—or even more often—than traditional medicine. Similar studies also indicate that the people who use alternative remedies rarely discuss them with their mainstream physician.

A growing number of health-care providers, specialists, and researchers use both mainstream and alternative techniques, an approach called "integrative" or "complementary-alternative medicine" (CAM). But I know of relatively few people who can knowledgeably integrate the fields of voice medicine and CAM. Understanding and treating the voice are relatively new even in traditional medicine, and in my experience, few alternative-health practitioners seem knowledgeable in this specific area.

The good news is that recent changes in the funding of health-care research, and the open-mindedness of younger medical researchers, are improving our knowledge about how well alternative-health practices actually work and for what conditions. Some laryngologists include CAM in their recommendations, and in time there will likely be more crossover knowledge to help vocalists.

In this small health guide, it is impossible to review all the possible benefits and risks of the many alternative or non-traditional health-care practices and practitioners. Several books on the subject are listed in the References section.

<u>Mix and Match</u>

As a broad generalization, traditional Western medicine may be best at diagnosis—determining and naming what is wrong. Its solutions are typically specific and symptom-related. Alternative approaches, often termed "whole-person" or holistic, may examine and/or treat many aspects of the person and lifestyle, and their benefits may be slower or more subtle.

So one "complimentary" approach would be to see an experienced laryngologist to diagnose your voice problems and use what the doctor recommends to recover from the immediate problem. Then, explore non-traditional methods to support or deepen your healing process. *If you use alternative therapies, tell the physician about them to avoid negative or unexpected interactions between the two medical systems.*

Subconscious beliefs about healing systems—and about yourself—have been shown to have a strong influence on whether any treatment is effective. You are most likely to receive lasting benefit from a health-care approach that you believe in and that is offered by a doctor or healer with whom you feel comfortable.

Sound Mind, Sound Body

When we are highly stressed, depressed, anxious, or pessimistic and convinced of our powerlessness, our bodies are less resistant to illness and less able to repair the normal wear and tear of daily life. Optimism, a reliable family or social network, and some type of private contemplation, have all been proven to benefit the body in measurable ways.

The voice bears the same health risks as other cells and organs. If we are under chronic stress, not sleeping well, coping with changing relationships, or afraid of losing a job, the body's mechanisms for routine repair, cellular maintenance, and immune responses to infection may be compromised.

Optimistic affirmation, visualization, counseling, meditation, and similar mental interventions are now used in many medical settings to enhance treatment. Elite athletes regularly use mental rehearsal, imagery, and other psychological tools to improve their muscle coordination, speed, stamina, and competitive edge. These practices may help vocalists as well by reducing anxiety, reducing the internal distress when vocal difficulties arise, and helping you to stay hopeful during the course of treatment.

Chapter Eight Supplement

HERBS OF INTEREST

This information is provided for educational purposes only. It comes from respected publications in the field of herbal medicine, with added comments from my personal experience. Nothing here is intended to diagnose or treat any disease or condition in the individual reader. Please consult with a qualified, licensed health-care provider.

Aloe Vera Gel
Benefit: Gel form can be soothing to stomach, protective against acid reflux.
Caution: Avoid "latex" or "juice" forms of aloe, which are stronger and tend to give digestive cramps.

Cayenne Pepper
Benefit: Warming to throat and stomach; common in many styles of cooking.
Caution: If heartburn or GERD exist, cayenne makes them worse and should be avoided.

Chamomile
Benefit: Relaxing, calms anxiety, and can be soothing to digestion.
Caution: Don't use if you have ragweed allergies.

Echinacea
Benefit: Recent clinical research indicates no benefit.
Caution: Traditionally described as helping the body resist colds and flu, but considered risky for long-term use. Even those who believe it to be beneficial should not take this herb for more than 2 weeks at a time.

Garlic
Benefit: May shorten the duration of colds & flu.
Caution: Any "dose" large to have benefit may have socially unacceptable odor.

Ginger
Benefit: Relieves nausea, warms throat and stomach without aggravating heartburn.
Caution: None

Lemon Balm (Melissa)
Benefit: Calming, relieves anxiety.
Caution: May decrease alertness, speed of thought and reflexes.

Licorice Root
Benefit: Protective of stomach lining; temporarily soothing to throat.
Caution: Unprocessed forms increase blood pressure, so look for "DGL" formulation.

Marshmallow
Benefit: Gargle or drink tea for relief of cough, sore throat; some protective effect on stomach.
Caution: None

Peppermint
Benefit: Tea can help relieve nasal congestion.
Caution: Active ingredient menthol, common in throat lozenges, is irritating to larynx when inhaled. Mint worsens acid reflux because it relaxes the digestive system, including the valves at top & bottom of esophagus. Small amounts in toothpaste or mouthwash may be tolerated.

Sage
Benefit: Traditional remedy for sore throats, fever.
Caution: Strong flavor is difficult as tea, but does nicely in chicken or vegetable soup.

Slippery Elm
Benefit: Helps tissues hold fluid, feels soothing to sore throats. Possible anti-inflammatory properties.

Caution: Commercial formulation "Throat Coat" tea contains licorice, risky if you have high blood pressure.

Tea (Black/Green)

Benefit: Relieves chest congestion; general health effect from antioxidants.
Caution: See caffeine discussions; green or white tea are usually milder than black.

Valerian

Benefit: Relaxing, anti-anxiety, sedative.
Caution: Long-term use not studied. Strong flavor may be disagreeable; may alter dreams.

Those who think they have not time for bodily exercise will sooner or later have to find time for illness.

Edward Stanley (1799–1869)

Chapter Nine

EXERCISE

As I state often in this book, the voice is an instrument within the body, and it reflects the overall health of the body. So in general, the vitality, resilience, and mental benefits of exercise are probably more important for vocalists than for the average person. In fact, the first popularity of jogging in the 1970s came from the enthusiasm of opera singers.

Many voice students I know, like other citizens of our fast-paced modern world, find it hard to get the regular exercise recommended by health experts, even if they may personally enjoy it. It is that much more important to use your time well and engage in physical activities that can best support vocal health.

Traditional sports, such as swimming, running, soccer, and basketball, as well as dance and aerobics classes, help build stamina and strong, efficient breathing. Notice, though, that during sports or dance activities, you focus on what's happening around you.

By contrast, vocal activity happens in the center of the body and is largely out of sight. The external focus and clear physicality of dance and athletics may be a welcome break from the intensity of voice work. Just be aware of the differences, so you can shift your focus and perspective as needed.

The most fundamental difference between voice and most aerobic activities is in breath rhythm: in-fast/out-slow for voice as opposed to relatively equal in/out timing during most physical fitness and sports activities. So these activities may well strengthen your breathing muscles, but only a few reinforce the specific breath use needed for voice. See the listing at the end of this chapter for details.

Mind and Body Together

As I explained earlier, the voice works inside the breath system, and it is controlled in ways that are not totally conscious. Therefore, the best forms of physical exercise for vocalists are those that integrate the body, mind, and breath, helping to harmonize conscious and unconscious functions.

With this goal in mind, my favorite exercises come from Tai Chi Chuan, Chi Gong, and the movement methods developed by Moishe Feldenkrais. I encourage you to explore these approaches to body awareness and conditioning. Practiced regularly, they can support vocal training in profound and subtle ways.

Popular again after thousands of years of history, yoga is great for posture, physical relaxation, flexibility, and concentration. See the supplement at the end of this chapter.

The Alexander Technique is often recommended for vocalists. It was developed by an injured actor and orator, and it retrains unconscious muscle habits with a special focus on head and neck alignment. It is sometimes used as an aid to rehabilitation of acute vocal injuries. As a quiet, mostly mental discipline, Alexander lessons are best balanced by more vigorous aerobic activities.

> It is exercise alone that supports the spirits, and keeps the mind in vigor.
> *Marcus Tullius Cicero (106 - 43 BC)*

Play Hard, Take Care

Those who coach athletics, especially outdoors, are at high risk for vocal strain and overuse injuries. As much as possible, save your voice for meaningful communication rather than long-distance signaling. Use a whistle to get players' attention and a megaphone or portable microphone and speaker to project and protect your voice.

Cheerleaders and athletes expected to shout during the game should warm up their voices as well as their bodies. Limit how much you talk over noise at post-game parties, and steam your throat as often as you ice your muscle aches.

Whatever your favorite sport or fitness activity, protect your voice. *Don't* lift any weight so heavy you have to hold your breath or grunt. *Don't* shout over loud music just because a fitness teacher wants you to. *Do* pay attention to your breathing during exercise, and find creative ways to develop the swift, silent inhalation and longer, smoothly controlled exhalation you'll want for your voice.

After every workout, take time to stretch your neck, back, shoulders, chest, and the muscles around your rib cage. Stretch your abdominal muscles and learn how to relax as well as tighten them.

Finally, a regular weekly or monthly professional massage is very helpful for relaxation and mind-body integration. Massage facilities and spas often have steam rooms, an added vocal boost.

> We seek not rest but transformation.
> Marge Piercy (1936 -)

Chapter Nine Supplement

FITNESS ACTIVITIES

Abdominal Exercise

Benefits: Posture, appearance, breath awareness. Keeps back healthy and strong.

Cautions: Don't hold your breath during these (or any other) exercises.

Other comments: Breathe as silently as possible. After the workout, stretch and relax the abdominal area as carefully as you strengthened it.

Aerobic Conditioning ("Cardio "): running, bicycling, treadmill, stair steps, etc.

Benefits: Heart-lung fitness; process oxygen efficiently; strengthen entire respiratory system.

Cautions: Vigorous upper-chest expansion on inhalation may be necessary in high-intensity exercise; not as desirable when vocalizing. In biking and spinning, oblique abdominals may become over-trained and the back of neck tight.

Other comments: Explore short intervals of asymmetrical breathing (in-fast/out-slow) during any aerobic workout to support the rhythm and control needed for voice.

Dance

Benefits: Cardio conditioning; posture, flexibility, appearance. Trains the body to respond to music.

Cautions: Don't talk, yell, or teach over loud music without a microphone. Posture and breathing techniques for dance are not the same as for voice; singing dancers must learn to adjust breath to suit each activity.

Other comments: Imagine throat wide open (silent) on inhalation. Occasionally relax/soften abdomen to keep space available for vocal support.

Martial Arts

Benefits: Aerobic fitness, flexibility, mind-body connection, subtle energy circulation, "soft-belly" with low center of gravity.

Cautions: May require shouts and grunts that can harm the voice over time.

Swimming

Benefits: Typically uses "in-fast/out-slow" breath rhythm, very similar to vocal performance. *Possibly the best exercise activity for voice professionals.*

Cautions: Keep neck relaxed. Chlorine in water is irritating to some people, leading to a sore-throat feeling. Discuss with your doctor.

Other comments: If facility has a steam room, use it!

Sports (indoor or outdoor, solo or team)

Benefits: Fitness, stress management, teamwork.

Cautions: Sports postures that constantly position the neck (such as surfing, spinning) can put strain on the voice mechanism.

Other comments: Limit shouting, yelling, cheering, coaching. Stretch thoroughly after the workout or game, and take advantage of steam-room facilities. Limit alcohol and talking over noise at post-game parties.

Strength Training (calisthenics, weights)

Benefits: Overall fitness, joint support, injury recovery, endurance, appearance.

Cautions: Don't hold your breath, even if that means lifting less weight. Don't engage neck muscles while working other body parts.

Other comments: Don't exhale *on* exertion, start exhaling *before* the push. After strengthening muscles of the neck, shoulders, chest, abdomen, sides, or back, spend generous time stretching them out for maximum freedom and ease of movement.

Tai Chi, Chi Gong

Benefits: Low-impact aerobic fitness, flexibility, mind-body connection, subtle-energy circulation, "soft-belly" with low center of gravity.

Cautions: Some specialized Chi Gong healing techniques involve tightening the throat muscles to hold breath and "compress" the air in the body. If you practice this, be sure to relax the throat fully afterwards.

Other comments: These are among the best forms of fitness exercise for voice; highly recommended.

Yoga

Benefits: Fully expansive breathing, mindfulness and subtle-body awareness, relaxation, flexibility, unity of mind-body-breath.

Cautions: Yoga breathing is different than voice technique in rhythm and purpose; they may complement each other but are not the same.

- Deliberately constricted, audible "Ujaya" breathing can be stressful to the voice or not, depending on the way it is done and the experience of the teacher. When in doubt, keep your breathing silent to protect vocal folds from dryness and fatigue.

- The head stand, shoulder stand, plough, fish, and similar poses that emphasize the neck should be avoided after any kind of vocal surgery. Wait at least a month or until your doctor says it is safe to return to them (ask!).

Other comments:

- Use back-bending postures (cobra, bow, bridge)to lengthen the abdominal muscles after calisthenics or crunches.
- Use meditation and visualization practices to help overcome stage fright and help your voice recover from injury.
- See Melton & Tom's book *One Voice*, in References, for an excellent chapter on yoga and voice training.

I'll view the manners of the town,
Peruse the traders, gaze upon the buildings,
And then return and sleep within mine inn,
For with long travel I am stiff and weary.
William Shakespeare
The Comedy of Errors

Chapter Ten

TRAVEL

Travel (especially by air) brings its own vocal risks. The biggest challenges that I hear about from patients and doctors are hydration, sleep, food (reflux), overuse, and not noticing problems soon enough because of the distractions or pressures of unfamiliar environments and routines.

If money is tight or your travel arrangements are made by agencies, tour managers, or other staff, you may not have ideal control of your working and living conditions when away from home. Do what you can to protect your voice, and use the general ideas behind these guidelines to create solutions of your own.

<u>Hydration</u>

The passenger cabin of an airplane has been described as dryer than the Sahara Desert. Some symptoms of jet lag may actually be dehydration. Meanwhile, as I've already emphasized, the vocal instrument fatigues without enough water held in the body and enough moisture in the air. So you need to take extra precautions to keep your airway humidified and your body adequately nourished with fluids.

It used to be simple to recommend that vocal profession-als drink plenty of water before, during, and after air travel. Recent changes in security rules make it less convenient to bring beverages with you. If you can, purchase a bottle of water inside the security zone.

Another idea is to bring an empty bottle in your carry-on bag and ask a flight attendant to fill it with water as soon as convenient. Instead of preparing your favorite tea in a thermos, bring your tea bags with you and request hot water for brewing. Remember to limit caffeine as well as alcoholic drinks when you're in the air, as their diuretic effects will make dehydration worse.

To hydrate your airway, there are some over-the-counter sprays and gels that help keep the inside of the nose moist. Another tip I've used is to carry a damp washcloth or handkerchief in a small plastic bag and take it out to breathe through from time to time. On long flights, just remoisten it in the lavatory.

When you land, refill your water bottle and continue to sip frequently. As soon as possible after you arrive where you will be staying, take a long shower and inhale the steam.

Sleep

Simple fatigue can lead to vocal strain. Travel with ear plugs, a light-blocking eye mask, and other comforts that help you sleep soundly while traveling.

Again, drinking coffee and alcoholic beverages during your trip may seem like well-deserved relief from the inevitable fatigue, disorientation, loneliness, and unexpected difficulties of travel. But these substances make it harder to sleep. Avoid or limit them, especially while on the road, and you'll be more likely to get enough sleep—the deepest refreshment of all.

Reflux on the Road

Travel schedules can disrupt your best intentions to control and diminish acid reflux. But a little planning goes a long way.

If you take reflux medications, talk to your doctor about how to stay on schedule with them as you change time zones and deal with irregular meal schedules. Keep some of your medication with you on the plane/train/tour bus, rather than putting all of it in your heavier luggage. That way, you're prepared for schedule changes or unexpected meals.

Bring extra medication with you in case your travel is extended for several days. And no matter how your eating schedule changes in different time zones or cultures, do your best to avoid eating or drinking heavily right before going to sleep.

Overuse

A primary reason for travel is to communicate directly with friends, family, business associates, and/or audiences you don't otherwise see. These are all temptations to overuse your voice.

Don't waste your voice—save it for your performance and most important conversations. Avoid speaking over noise, choose social activities with care, and listen more than you talk.

If you are recovering from a vocal problem and have been advised to rest or limit voice use, your needs may not be understood as easily as a visible injury like a broken bone. Strangers and people who haven't seen you in a while won't necessarily know—or remember—how to help you.

You may not want to compromise privacy or your professional image by revealing the full details of your dilemma. Nevertheless, while planning your trip, look for discreet ways to let key people know that you are paying attention to vocal care and that you have some new personal habits. Then stick to those limits as best you can.

Paying Attention

Daily diligence is your best protection against injury. No matter where or how you travel, look for ways to move and stretch your body, breathe easily, stay hydrated, sleep adequately, and rest your voice.

Warm up as attentively as when you are at home, even if there is less time. Use your warm-up to measure how well your voice is doing under the circumstances and whether you need to be even more careful with your precautions, especially if you're on an extended trip.

Consider keeping a travel log or diary about how your voice performs and solutions or strategies that seem most helpful. This will also help you remember problems or questions to discuss with your teacher, doctor, or voice therapist when you get home.

Chapter Ten Supplement

TRUE NOTES FROM THE ROAD

MUSICIAN'S DIARY, Tuesday, 7 p.m.
Twilight. Drizzle. Been driving all day. Three frustrating hours stuck behind a bad freeway accident put me way behind schedule. Played a coffeehouse last night; tomorrow I've got a radio promo and a full-length concert in the back room of a music store.

I pull off the Interstate, fumble for my itinerary and cell phone. Tell the friend who's hosting me that I won't make it for supper. Get out to stretch my legs, then grind down the highway for three or four more hours. I'll keep the radio off for awhile, do some breathing exercises and then vocalize.

Midnight, at the oasis (finally!)
I found a parking space only a block away from where I'm staying, and lugged my stuff up to my friends' third-floor apartment. Played with their new dog while they briefed me on the schedule for tomorrow. It looks like I'll be able to get some decent sleep and have time for yoga stretches and a solid warm-up between brunch and the radio broadcast. Later, we'll swing by the music store for sound check, then back to base camp for a shower, light supper, and performance prep.

Wednesday, 5 p.m.
Still gray and drizzling. Sound check introduced me to the mic stand from hell: an aging gooseneck that droops out of position on a whim. Fixing it and finding a buzz-free monitor took longer than I'd planned. So I can't take half an hour to choose my earrings.

Thursday, 10 a.m..
Gig drew well despite the bad weather. The guy at the coffee bar next door donated a thermos of herb tea, and my voice stayed clear. Sold almost as many CDs as I'd hoped, then celebrated (quietly) with the local pals who made it all happen.
...Now I'm back behind the wheel. Today's distance quota is like that old railroad ballad: 500 miles. Despite my best efforts, I'm definitely more tired than when I left home two weeks ago. If I stay disciplined, I will finish this marathon. But please, no more traffic accidents! I want that in my contract.

Excerpted from "Planes, Trains, and Vocal Fatigue" by Joanna Cazden, *Electronic Musician* August 1998. Full article at www.voiceofyourlife.com

The moment we begin to fear the opinions
of others and hesitate to tell the truth that is
in us, and from motives of policy [we] are
silent when we should speak, the divine
floods of light and life no longer flow into our
souls.

Elizabeth Cady Stanton (1815-1902)

Chapter Eleven

INTANGIBLES

The Voice of Your Life

Creating the sounds of singing or speech unites all the essential elements of life. Using one's voice and being heard by others is an amazing biological act. It is also an important expression of life, freedom, spirituality, individuality, and community.

If your voice is struggling, it may be normal to experience the problem as simultaneously personal and interpersonal, deeply private yet impossible to hide. When my speech-therapy clients lose their voices completely, or are advised for medical reasons to rest in silence as much as possible, they are often astounded at how deeply this changes their relationships and their place in the world.

It may be impossible to fully care for the voice without acknowledging the subtler dimensions of its meaning. When circumstances require us to withhold important truths, to keep silent when we long to shout for attention or for justice, the block may be felt physically as a "lump in the throat." But when we say things that are true, "sing from the heart," or find the courage to "speak truth to power" as the Quakers put it, the voice may carry its greatest power and richness of sound.

This is not to imply that vocal problems are "all in your head." But if your voice develops a problem, consider whether there is a hidden message, some part of *you* that is struggling to be "heard." Paradoxically, vocal rest can be a time for listening to the "inner voice," inviting unexpected truths to make themselves known from within.

Wellness in the World

Similarly, when things are going well, a healthy vocal sound indicates to others that your body, mind, and spirit are balanced, integrated, vibrant, and expressive. Your voice, like other parts of your individual nature, is unique in human existence, and its capacity is worth developing and protecting.

Be gentle and realistic with yourself as you learn to care for your voice. Seek appropriate professional care, then find the time and support to design strategic changes in lifestyle and voice use that fit you as an individual.

Balanced nutrition, exercise, rest, satisfying relationships, and an authentic, optimistic spirit are good for your overall health and good for your voice. Let your desire for a healthy voice help motivate you to take good care of your body and mind and to build a life and lifestyle that support and express your unique self.

Lift every voice and sing
     till earth and heaven ring,
Ring with the harmonies of liberty.
Let our rejoicing rise
     high as the listening skies;
Let it resound loud as the rolling sea.
               James Weldon Johnson (1871–1938)

REFERENCES

Resources and Suggested Reading

ONLINE RESOURCES

Disclaimer: Websites change quickly; no guarantee is made about the availability or accuracy of information sites on this list.

To Find a Laryngologist:

(USA)
National Voice Center Referral list
www.gbmc.org/voice/national.cfm

(CANADA, AUSTRALIA)
www.gbmc.org/voice/national.cfm#international

(USA & WORLDWIDE)
www.entlink.net/international/societies/

Some Vocal Health Information Sites

A 2 Z Vocal Health
www.A2ZVocalHealth.com

Greater Baltimore Medical Center's Voice Center
www.gbmc.org/voice/index.cfm

Laryngology information for the public
www.entlink.net/news/World-Voice-Day-Fact-Sheets.cfm

Live Science: 10 Tips for a Healthy Voice.
www.livescience.com/humanbiology/060417_voice_tips

National Center for Voice and Speech
www.ncvs.org

University of Pittsburgh Voice Center
www.pitt.edu/~crosen/voice

The Voice Problem Website
www.voiceproblem.org

Voice Academy (for school teachers)
www.uiowa.edu/~shcvoice/

The Voice Foundation
www.voicefoundation.org

Voice and Speech Trainers Association
** offers its own, excellent, online resources list
www.vasta.org/weblinks7.html

Warm-Up Exercises Online

www.voiceguy.blogspot.com

www.entlink.net/news/voiceday_warmup.cfm

Voice Teacher Directories

Many voice teachers advertise on the web individually. Those who belong to the organizations below are more likely to have continued their own education, and they have agreed to follow the codes of ethics or practice principles published by the organization. Always use your own judgment when meeting a new teacher. It is common to take a "sample lesson" with a teacher—or several teachers—before committing yourself to extended study. Just say so up front!

National Association of Teachers of Singing (NATS)
www.nats.org/find_teacher.php

Voice and Speech Trainers Association (VASTA)
www.vasta.org/professional_index/index_by_state.html

SELECTED BOOKS

Voice Production, Care, and Training

Abitbol, J. (2006). *Odyssey of the Voice.* Translated by Patricia Crossley. Plural Publishing Inc.

Baxter, M. (1991). *The Rock-N-Roll Singer's Survival Manual.* Hal Leonard Publishing Corporation.

Boren, M. (2005). *Breathing for Performance: A Guide for Wind and Voice Musicians.* Powerlung Press.

Eisenson, J. & Eisenson, A.M. (1991). *Voice and Diction: A Program for Improvement, 6th edition.* Prentice Hall.

Hixon, Thomas J. (2007). *Respiratory Function in Singing: A Primer for Singers And Singing Teachers.* Redington Brown & Co.

Horwitz, B. (2002). *Communication Apprehension: Origins and Management.* Singular Thomson Learning.

Lamperti, G. B. (1957). *Vocal Wisdom.* Translated from the French and edited by Strongin, L. & Brown, W. Taplinger Publishing Company.

Lessac, A. (1967). *The Use and Training of the Human Voice.* Drama Books.

Linklater, K. (1976). *Freeing the Natural Voice.* Drama Books.

Martin, S. & Darnley, L. (1992). *The Voice Sourcebook.* Winslow Press.

Melton, J. & Tom, K. (2003). *One Voice: Integrating Singing Technique and Theatre Voice Training.* Heinemann.

Miller, F.E. (2003). *The Voice: Its Production, Care and Preservation.* Kessinger Publishing.

Miller, R. (2003). *Solutions for Singers: Tools for Performers and Teachers.* Oxford University Press

Pinksterboer, H. (2003). *Vocals: The Singing Voice (Tipbook).* Hal Leonard Publications.

Ristad, E. (1982). *A Soprano On Her Head: Right-Side-Up Reflections on Life and Other Performances.* Real People Press.

Rodenburg, P. (1992). *The Right To Speak.* Methuen.

Thurman, L. & Welch, G., co-editors. (2000). *Bodymind & Voice: Foundations of Voice Education,* revised edition. National Center for Voice and Speech.

Verdolini, K. (1998). *Guide to Vocology.* National Center for Voice and Speech.

Body, Mind, and Breath

Brostoff, J. & Gamlin, L. (2000). *Asthma: The Complete Guide to Integrative Therapies.* Healing Arts Press.

Gagnon, D. et al. (1990). *Breathe Free: Nutritional and Herbal Care for Your Respiratory System.* Lotus Press.

Kabat-Zinn, J. (2006). *Coming to Our Senses: Healing Ourselves and the World Through Mindfulness.* Hyperion Books.

Mayo Clinic (2007). *Mayo Clinic Book of Alternative Medicine: The New Approach to Using the Best of Natural Therapies and Conventional Medicine*. Time Inc. Home Entertainment.

Murray, M. (1998). *Encyclopedia of Natural Medicine 2nd Edition*. Three Rivers Press.

Phaneuf, H. (2005). *Herbs Demystified: A Scientist Explains How the Most Common Herbal Remedies Really Work*. Marlowe & Company.

Saraswati, Swami Charmananda (1966). *Breath of Life*. Motilal Banarsidass Publishers Pvt. Ltd. (www.mlbd.com)

Schachter, N. (2006). *The Good Doctor's Guide to Colds and Flu*. Harper Torch.

Tierra, M. (1988). *Planetary Herbology*. Lotus Press.

Weil, A. (1983). *Health and Healing*. Houghton Mifflin.

_____ (2004). *Natural Health, Natural Medicine: The Complete Guide to Wellness and Self-Care for Optimum Health*. Houghton Mifflin.

SCIENTIFIC & TECHNICAL REFERENCES

American Speech-Language-Hearing Association. (2005). *The role of the speech-language pathologist, the teacher of singing, and the speaking voice trainer in voice habilitation* (technical report). Available from www.asha.org.

Boekema, P.J., Samsom, M., Smout, A.J. (1999). Effect of coffee on gastro-oesophageal reflux in patients with reflux disease and healthy controls. *Eur J Gastroenterol Hepatol.* 11(11):1271-6.

Brazer, S.R., Onken, J.E., Dalton, C.B., Smith, J.W., Schiffman, S.S. (1995). Effect of different coffees on esophageal acid contact time and symptoms in coffee-sensitive subjects. *Physiol Behav.* Mar;57(3):563-7.

Brinckmann, J., et al. (2003). Safety and efficacy of a traditional herbal medicine (Throat Coat) in symptomatic temporary relief of pain in patients with acute pharyngitis: a multicenter, prospective, randomized, double-blinded, placebo-controlled study. *J Altern Complement Med.* Apr;9(2):285-98.

Brody, J.E. (2007). "You are also what you drink." *New York Times,* 3/27 (www.nytimes.com).

Edgar, J.D. (2007). "Is Singing More Difficult After Eating a Meal?" *Journal of Singing* (63), 4, pp. 431-439.

El-Serag, H.B., Satia, J.A., Rabeneck, L. (2005). Dietary intake and the risk of gastro-oesophageal reflux disease: a cross sectional study *Gut.* Jan;54(1):11-7.

Ford, C.N. (2005). Evaluation and management of laryngo-pharyngeal reflux. *JAMA.* Sep 28;294(12):1534-40.

Grandjean, A.C., Reimers, K.J., Bannick, K.E., Haven, M.C. (2000). The effect of caffeinated, non-caffeinated, caloric, and non-caloric beverages on hydration. *J Am Coll Nutr.* Oct;19(5):591-600.

Hindmarch, I., Rigney, U., Stanley, N., Quinlan, P., Rycroft, J., Lane, J. (2000). A naturalistic investigation of the effects of day-long consumption of tea, coffee, and water on alertness, sleep onset and sleep quality. *Psychopharmacology (Berl).* Apr;149(3):203-16.

Kaltenbach, T., Crockett, S., Gerson, L.B. (2006). Are lifestyle measures effective in patients with gastroesophageal reflux disease? An evidence-based approach. *Arch Intern Med.* May 8;166(9):965-71.

Khan, A.M., Hashmi, S.R., Elahi, F., Tariq, M., Ingrams, D.R. (2006). Laryngopharyngeal reflux: A literature review. *Surgeon.* Aug;4(4):221-5.

Koufman, J.A. (2002). Laryngopharyngeal reflux is different from classic gastroesophageal reflux disease. *Ear Nose Throat J.* Sep;81(9 Suppl 2):7-9.

Leonard, R., Kendall, K. (2001) Phonoscopy-A Valuable Tool for Otolaryngologists and Speech-Language Pathologists in the Management of Dysphonic Patients. *The Laryngoscope: Volume 111*(10) pp 1760-1766

Lipan, M.J., Reidenberg, J.S., Laitman, J.T. (2006). Anatomy of reflux: a growing health problem affecting structures of the head and neck. *The Anatomical Record Part B: The New Anatomist* Nov; 289(6):261-70.

Nilsson, M., Johnsen, R., Ye, W., Hveem, K., Lagergren, J. (2004). Lifestyle related risk factors in the aetiology of gastro-oesophageal reflux. *Gut.* Dec;53(12):1730-5.

Riesenhuber, A., Boehm, M., Posch, M., Aufricht, C. (2006). Diuretic potential of energy drinks. *Amino Acids.* Jul;31(1):81-3. Epub (2006) Jun 1.

Stookey, J.D. (1999). The diuretic effects of alcohol and caffeine and total water intake misclassification. *Eur J Epidemiol.* Feb;15(2):181-8.

Terry, P., Lagergren, J., Wolk, A., Nyren, O. (2000). Reflux-inducing dietary factors and risk of adenocarcinoma of the esophagus and gastric cardia. *Nutr Cancer.*;38(2):186-91.

Watts, C. & Rousseau, B (2008). The Biochemistry of Slippery Elm (Ulmus Rubra) and its Use as a Complimentary and Alternative Medicine. The Voice Foundation: 37th Annual Symposium on Care of the Professional Voice, Philadelphia PA.

Wendl, B., Pfeiffer, A., Pehl, C., Schmidt, T., Kaess, H. (1994). Effect of decaffeination of coffee or tea on gastro-oesophageal reflux. *Aliment Pharmacol Ther.* Jun;8(3):283-7.

He who sings frightens away his ills.
Miguel de Cervantes (1547–1616)

Lightning Source UK Ltd.
Milton Keynes UK
08 October 2009

144727UK00001B/11/P